GOD'S LAW
IN THE
MODERN WORLD

Other books by Kenneth L. Gentry, Jr.

The Christian Case Against Abortion, 1982, rev. 1989

The Christian and Alcoholic Beverages: A Biblical Perspective, 1986

The Charismatic Gift of Prophecy: A Reformed Response to Wayne Grudem, 1986, rev. 1989

The Beast of Revelation, 1989

Before Jerusalem Fell: Dating the Book of Revelation, 1989

House Divided: The Break-up of Dispensational Theology (with Greg L. Bahnsen), 1989

The Greatness of the Great Commission: The Christian Enterprise in a Fallen World, 1990

He Shall Have Dominion: A Postmillennial Eschatology, 1992

Lord of the Saved: Getting to the Heart of the Lordship Debate, 1992

GOD'S LAW IN THE MODERN WORLD

THE CONTINUING RELEVANCE OF OLD TESTAMENT LAW

KENNETH L. GENTRY, JR.

INSTITUTE FOR CHRISTIAN ECONOMICS
TYLER, TEXAS

Unless otherwise indicated, Scripture quotations are from *The Holy Bible, New King James Version*. Copyright © 1979, 1980, 1982 by Thomas Nelson, Inc. Nashville, Tennessee.

Manufactured in the United States of America

Library of Congress Cataloging-in-Publications Data

Gentry, Kenneth L.
    God's law in the modern world : the continuing relevance of Old Testament law / Kenneth L. Gentry, Jr.
        p.   cm.
    Includes index.
    ISBN 0-930464-77-X
    1. Law (Theology) 2. Law (Theology)—Biblical teaching. 3. Bible. O.T.—Theology. 4. Dominion theology.
I. Title.
BT96.2.G45   1993
241.5—dc20   92-36051

CONTENTS

PREFACE

Those who promote the applicability of God's Law in the modern world are often written off without a hearing. Two pragmatic considerations tend to dominate theological discussions of the Law.

On the one hand, Law advocacy represents a call to a radical commitment to the Word of God in *every* area of life, and that is out of step with both fundamentalism and modern evangelicalism. Theologically, fundamentalism tends to be both pietistic (dwelling on the inner personal life and the private Christian walk) and retreatist (withdrawing from a consideration of the large social issues). On the other hand, neo-evangelicalism tends to be faddish (being drawn, belatedly, into the secular humanist cultural wake) and ambivalent (too prone to "reinterpret" the Scripture when it runs contrary to contemporary "science").

Those who advance God's Law in modern ethical discourse are calling Christians to consider the larger issues of life for the historical long run, as well as the personal questions of the daily Christian walk. But the fundamentalist's doctrine of the any-moment coming of Christ discourages such a long-range view. "Why polish brass on a sinking ship?" Proponents of the Law of God call upon the Christian not only to consider the implications of the Christian faith for the larger question of a Christian culture, but also to act upon that consideration from a biblical perspective. But that is too antiquarian and naive for the neo-evangelical. Advocates of a Bible-based ethic demand deep biblical study and committed, determinative action. And all of this in an age of comfortable pews.

Furthermore, since defenders of God's Law issue a clarion call to Christian commitment in all of life, those Christians who do not adopt such an ethic quite naturally fear it. That is because when any position is to your right, then you are to its left. That is a constant source of embarrassment both to retreatist fundamentalism and to status-quo evangelical Christianity, both of which prefer not to appear on the left. The large cultural questions are simply not treated from a rigorously Bible-based perspective in modern Christendom. Thus advocates of the Law of God are put down without careful and reflective thought. The popular writings of Hal Lindsey and Dave Hunt are classic illustrations of such incautious pietism.[1] And even the response by Westminster Theological Seminary to the modern employment of God's Law does not speak adequately to the issues.[2]

The purpose of this small work is briefly to introduce the reader in a nontechnical way to the case for the modern use of God's Law in ethics. The ethic that is rigorously based on God's Law is known as *theonomic ethics*. Because of the oftentimes complicated nature of the debate, many committed Christians who are sincerely interested in hearing the case presented from Scripture have felt at a loss for material to evaluate.

Fuller and more technical arguments for the general applicability of the Old Testament case laws for today may be found in Greg L. Bahnsen's *Theonomy in Christian Ethics* and *By This Standard*.[3] Specific applications of a number of the Old Testament case laws may be found in Gary North's *Tools of Dominion*[4] and R. J. Rushdoony's two volume *Institutes of Biblical Law*.[5]

It is hoped that this introductory study of the case for theonomic ethics might minister to those who have not been able to wade through the larger more academic works on the subject.

I would like to thank Gary DeMar for his invaluable technical help in the production of this manuscript. His Christian labor is greatly appreciated.

NOTES

1. Hal Lindsey, *The Road to Holocaust* (New York: Bantam, 1989), and Dave Hunt, *Whatever Happened to Heaven?* (Portland, Oreg.: Harvest, 1989). See analysis of these books in conjunction with another work, in Kenneth L. Gentry, Jr., and Greg L. Bahnsen, *House Divided: The*

Break-up of Dispensational Theology (Tyler, Tex.: Institute for Christian Economics, 1989).

2. William S. Barker and W. Robert Godfrey, *Theonomy: A Reformed Critique* (Grand Rapids: Zondervan, 1990). For critiques, see Gary North, *Westminster's Confession: The Abandonment of Van Til's Legacy* (Tyler, Tex.: Institute for Christian Economics, 1991), Greg L. Bahnsen, *No Other Standard: Theonomy and Its Critics* (Tyler, Tex.: Institute for Christian Economics, 1991), and Gary North, ed., *Theonomy: An Informed Response* (Tyler, Tex.: Institute for Christian Economics, 1991).

3. Greg L. Bahnsen, *Theonomy in Christian Ethics*, 2d ed. (Phillipsburg, N.J.: Presbyterian and Reformed, 1984) and *By This Standard* (Tyler, Tex.: Institute for Christian Economics, 1985).

4. Gary North, *Tools of Dominion: The Case Laws of Exodus* (Tyler, Tex.: Institute for Christian Economics, 1990).

5. R. J. Rushdoony, *Institutes of Biblical Law* (Nutley, N.J.: Craig, 1973; reissued by Presbyterian and Reformed) and *Law and Society: Volume 2 of The Institutes of Biblical Law* (Vallecito, Calif.: Ross House, 1982).

CHAPTER ONE

INTRODUCTION

Evangelicals are reluctant to adopt controversial teachings, even those which can be shown to have biblical support. Sometimes it is helpful to see how others have come to embrace a position regarded as controversial. That being the case, I would like to present a brief testimony tracing my own route to theonomic ethics.

MY EARLY DISPENSATIONALISM

From 1966 until 1975 I was a dispensationalist, having been attracted to the movement because it boasted of a consistent biblical outlook that could explain the times. I was saved by the grace of the Lord Jesus Christ at a dispensationalist youth camp, attended a dispensationalist church, graduated with a degree in

Bible from a dispensationalist college (Tennessee Temple University), and attended a dispensationalist seminary (Grace Theological Seminary) for two years.

In many ways it was great being a dispensationalist, and yet it was also frustrating. It was great to be able to pinpoint the reason for the problems of modern society: man's sinful condition before God. It was frustrating that as a Christian I was not expected to have any biblical solutions to those problems. And this despite being taught that the earth is the Lord's and the gospel is the power of God unto salvation.

While studying at Grace Theological Seminary two influences converged that caused me to reject dispensationalism. The first was my researching a paper on the lordship controversy.[1] This led to my discovery of the significance of the Acts 2 enthronement passage, which shook my dispensationalism to its very foundation. The second was the discovery at about the same time of O. T. Allis's *Prophecy and the Church*. This work bulldozed the residue of my collapsed dispensationalism.[2] A couple of friends of mine (Rev. Alan McCall and Barry Bostrom) and I not only soon departed dispensationalism, but transferred from Grace Seminary to Reformed Theological Seminary in Jackson, Mississippi. Until then we had been partial Calvinists; now we had become more fully Reformed and hence nondispensational.

MY CONVERSION TO THEONOMIC ETHICS

At Reformed Seminary I took two courses that initially seemed implausible and misguided ex-

4

travagance. They were "History and Eschatology" (in which was set forth a postmillennial eschatology) and "Christian Theistic Ethics" (in which was set forth theonomic ethics). Both courses were taught by Dr. Greg L. Bahnsen.

Regarding the eschatological question, even though I was no longer a dispensationalist, I had assumed J. Dwight Pentecost, Hal Lindsey, and other dispensationalists were correct in declaring that "postmillennialism finds no defenders or advocates in the present chiliastic discussions within the theological world."[3] I was unaware that in the very era in which Pentecost's book was published (1958), there were at least four notable works in defense of postmillennialism—one of them endorsed by the famed, orthodox Old Testament scholar, O. T. Allis, who is often quoted in Pentecost's book. Those books were J. Marcellus Kik's, *Matthew Twenty-Four* (1948) and *Revelation Twenty* (1955), Roderick Campbell's *Israel and the New Covenant* (introduction by O. T. Allis, 1954), and Loraine Boettner's *The Millennium* (1957).[4]

Even more far-fetched to me than the idea of the victory of the gospel in history was the applicability of Old Testament law to modern culture. I had always thought that the phrase "We are not under law, but under grace" taught that we had no obligations to obey God's ethical standards. "That's the Old Testament!" was an easy (but fallacious) way to dismiss the Mosaic Law, which God frequently calls "My Law."[5] Unfortunately, dispensational constructs still limited my theological perspective.

I continued in steadfast opposition to Professor

Bahnsen through almost half of each of the aforementioned courses. You might say that I "kicked against the pricks." But in both courses I was eventually swayed by the sheer force of biblical exegesis and consistent theological analysis. I went into these courses an anti-theonomic amillennialist; I came out a theonomic postmillennialist.

My Reformed theology was becoming complete; with the Westminster Divines I could cite Old Testament case laws alongside of New Testament passages for divine insight into the resolution of moral issues. I could also turn to the Old and New Testament prophetic hope for a proper understanding of the gospel victory theme of eschatology. In short, I could apply the whole of Scripture to the whole of life in confident anticipation of all glory being Christ's in His world.

MY DISAPPOINTMENT WITH OBJECTIONS

There are many unjust and misguided criticisms of the theonomic ethic based on outlandish charges passed as valid criticisms. One critic recently wrote: "On the subject of the law reconstructionism[6] has got both legs bogged down in a vat of quickly-drying concrete. . . . The list of criminals awaiting execution is long: homosexuals, Baptists, swindlers and gatherers of sticks on the Lord's Day!"[7] He offered no documentation of this charge.

Dispensationalist H. Wayne House writes: "Nothing is more heinous in a theocratic society than to openly question the law-order. The legitimate institutions must therefore react with 'destruction' or other appropriate punishment to those with whom they are at war."[8] What is interesting about this statement is that it is based on a statement by R. J. Rushdoony that any civil order must impose sanctions against criminal actions, such as treason. House leaps to the unjustified conclusion that mere unbelief in Christ or adherence to dispensationalism would under a Christian theocratic government be considered treasonous!

The distortions rampant in the Reconstruction debate are terribly frustrating. A prominent Christian journalist once asked me if I were going to leave the Presbyterian Church in America for a more theonomic environment. My answer was and continues to be no! My denomination is Bible-believing, Presbyterian, and Reformed in its confessional and constitutional standards—and that is what provides the basis for both my pastoral ministry and my Reconstructionist views.

The PCA and Theonomic Ethics

In point of fact, the PCA has considered theonomy on a few occasions and has always allowed it. "The General Assembly affirm[s] that no particular view of the application of the judicial law for today should be made a basis for orthodoxy or excluded as heresy."[9] The PCA position has such a clear tolerance for theonomy that the General Assembly even rebuked a presbytery for delaying a man's ordination on the sole basis of his accepting theonomy.[10] On another occasion it adjudicated a case in favor of a particular theonomist who was wrongly denied ordination solely because of his theonomic sympathies.[11]

Later another situation arose in which the General Assembly was asked about the contemporary applicability of Deuteronomy 13. The answer of the committee to study the question leaned toward a nontheonomic position. But that was accompanied by a qualifying statement prohibiting an improper use of the report to the inquiring presbytery: "Since there are differences of opinion with regard to the application and 'general equity' of the various penal sanctions, this declaration shall not be used by the courts of the Church to bind the conscience of elders in the PCA."[12]

One of the more unusual rebuttals to theonomic ethics comes from Meredith G. Kline. In a surprisingly frank article he takes exception to the Westminster Confession, lamenting that "[theonomy] is in fact a revival of certain teachings contained in the Westminster Confession of Faith. . . . Ecclesiastical courts operating under the Westminster Confession of Faith are going to have their problems, therefore, if they should be of a mind to bring the Chalcedon [i.e., theonomic] aberration under their judicial scrutiny."[13] That paper has been carefully answered in an article by Greg L. Bahnsen.[14]

WHAT IS THEONOMY?

Before examining the biblical case for theonomic ethics, let us make sure we have clearly defined the issue at hand.

THE MEANING OF THE TERM

"Theonomy" is derived from a combination of two Greek words: *theos* ("God") and *nomos* ("law"). It simply means "God's Law." Broadly speaking the term describes the Christian ethical position that holds that God's Word determines what is right and wrong, rather than "natural law." More narrowly "theonomy" is generally understood to point out the righteousness and practicality of the Mosaic civil code for modern application.

DISTINCTIVES OF THEONOMIC THOUGHT

In summary, the distinctives of the theonomic ethic are at least six. Theonomy holds that Old Testament Law (often called "the Mosaic Law," but actually wider than the Mosaic Law code) is:

1. Binding (that is, we are obliged to obey it for our *sanctification*); and
2. Relevant (in that all our Lord does is governed by all-wisdom and all-knowledge, thus making His Word practical for all times and applicable for all situations),
3. When properly interpreted (taking into account the full significance, purpose, and situation of the original intent of the various laws individually considered), and
4. Properly applied (the flow of redemptive history must be taken into account and the New Testament precepts and principles must be given their full significance[15]).

9

5. Thus, the details of the Law are essential to Law-keeping (they form an essential part of the Law, as parts to the whole), and

6. Are meant to be equitably observed by man on the personal, social, and civil levels of human existence.

This, in short, is the theonomic ethic to which I subscribe as an evangelical, Reformed Christian. Let us now turn to a consideration of the case for theonomic ethics.

NOTES

1. Now published as *Lord of the Saved: Getting to the Heart of the Lordship Debate* (Phillipsburg, N.J.: Presbyterian and Reformed, 1992).

2. For a study of the postmillennial eschatological question against the backdrop of dispensationalism, see: Greg L. Bahnsen and Kenneth L. Gentry, Jr., *House Divided: The Break-up of Dispensational Theology* (Tyler, Tex.: Institute for Christian Economics, 1989), chaps. 9-16.

3. J. Dwight Pentecost, *Things to Come* (Grand Rapids: Zondervan, 1958), p. 387; see also Hal Lindsey, *The Late Great Planet Earth* (Grand Rapids: Zondervan, 1971), p. 176.

4. The two titles by Kik have since been combined into one volume, *An Eschatology of Victory* (Phillipsburg, N.J.: Presbyterian and Reformed, 1971). For more detailed information on this narrow historical question and for the biblical case for postmillennialism, see my *He Shall Have Dominion: A Postmillennial Eschatology* (Tyler, Tex.: Institute for Christian Economics, 1992).

5. House and Ice say emphatically that we must differentiate "God's law" from "the law of Moses." H. Wayne House and Thomas D. Ice, *Dominion Theology: Blessing Or Curse?* (Portland, Oreg.: Multnomah, 1988), p. 100. However, when we read the Old Testament Scriptures, we find that God shows a special jealousy and is adamant to maintain that the Law given through Moses is His Law. The Law of Moses is identified over and over as the Law of Jehovah: e.g., Deut. 30:10; Josh. 24:26; 2 Kings 10:31; 17:13; 21:8; 1 Chron. 22:12; 2 Chron. 6:16; 31:21; Ezra 7:6, 12, 14, 21; Neh. 8:8, 18; 9:3; 10:28, 29; Pss. 78:1; 81:4; 89:30; 119:34, 77, 92, 97, 109, 174; Isa. 1:10; Jer. 6:19; 9:13; 16:11; 26:4; 31:33; 44:10; 22:26; Dan. 6:5; Hos. 4:6; 8:1.

6. A "Reconstructionist" is one who holds to the applicability of God's Law to modern society and government, while holding at the same time to the postmillennial hope that promises that Christianity will win the world to Christ through the gospel, which is "the power of God unto salvation."

7. Erroll Hulse, "Reconstructionism, Restorationism or Puritanism," in *Reformation Today*, No. 116 (July/August 1990): 25.

8. House and Ice, *Dominion Theology*, p. 77.

9. *Minutes of the Seventh General Assembly of the Presbyterian Church in America* (1979), p. 195 ("Report on Theonomy").

10. *Minutes of the Ninth General Assembly of the Presbyterian Church in America* (1981), p. 145, section 7 ("Review and Control of Presbyteries Report").

11. *Minutes of the Tenth General Assembly of the Presbyterian Church in America* (1982), pp. 107ff. ("Lee, et al. v. Gulf Coast Presbytery"). The antipathy by some toward theonomy is noted in that decision: "It is the judgment of the Commission that [Teaching Elder] Donald C. Graham has helped to aggravate the problem of dissension over

'theonomy' by circulating materials which contain in-temperate language to certain members of Gulf Coast Presbytery" (p. 108).

12. *Minutes of the Eleventh General Assembly of the Presbyterian Church in America* (1983), p. 97 ("Advice of the Sub-Committee on Judicial Business").

13. Meredith G. Kline, "Comments on an Old-New Error: A Review Article," in *Westminster Theological Journal* 41 (Fall 1978): 173.

14. Greg L. Bahnsen, "M. G. Kline on Theonomic Politics: An Evaluation of His Reply," *The Journal of Christian Reconstruction* 6 (Winter 1979-80): 195ff.

15. The theonomic ethic holds that the New Testament is the conclusive revelation of God for man. If the New Testament repeals or annuls a particular law from God's Law either by precept or example, then that law is not longer binding in this era. But we hold that it is only God speaking in Scripture who has the authority to do so.

CHAPTER TWO

THE ESSENCE OF GOD'S LAW

The Scripture so defines the nature of God's Law as to suggest very strongly its continuing validity today. This may be seen from a variety of angles.

THE LAW'S NATURE

1. *The Law represents the presence of God.* Unique to the Law of God is that it was personally written by the finger of God. "And when He had made an end of speaking with him on Mount Sinai, He gave Moses two tablets of the Testimony, tablets of stone, written with the finger of God" (Ex. 31:18; see also Ex. 32:16; Deut. 4:13; 9:10; 10:4). The Law's remarkable origin, like the soul of Adam (Gen. 2:7), suggests its holy character.

2. The Law lies at the very heart of the new covenant. The new covenant, as recorded in Jeremiah 31:31-33, reads:

> "Behold, the days are coming," says the LORD, "when I will make a new covenant with the house of Israel and with the house of Judah— not according to the covenant that I made with their fathers in the day that I took them by the hand to bring them out of the land of Egypt, My covenant which they broke, though I was a husband to them," says the LORD. But this is the covenant that I will make with the house of Israel: After those days, says the LORD, I will put *My law*[1] in their minds, and write it on their hearts; and I will be their God, and they shall be My people." (Emphasis added.)

The new covenant was put into effect with the establishment of the Lord's Supper just before the crucifixion of Christ.[2] We live today under the new covenant administration of redemption and are reminded of that every time we partake of the Lord's Supper.

3. The Law reflects God's character. When we survey the scriptural representations of the character of God's Law, we soon discover that the same moral attributes applied to it are also used in reference to the very being of God. God is good (Mark 10:18; Ps. 143:10); the Law is good (Deut. 12:28; Ps. 119:68; Rom. 7:12, 16). God is holy (Isa. 6:3; Rev. 15:4); the Law is holy (Num. 15:40; Rom. 7:12). God is perfect (2 Sam. 22:31; Ps. 18:30; Matt. 5:48); the Law is perfect (Ps. 1:25; James 1:25). God is spiritual (John 4:24); the Law is spiritual

(Rom. 7:14). God is righteous (Deut. 32:4; Ezra 9:15; Ps. 116:5); the Law is righteous (Deut. 4:8; Ps. 19:7; Rom. 2:26; 8:4). God is just (Deut. 32:4; Ps. 25:8, 10; Isa. 45:21); the Law is just (Prov. 28:4, 5; Zech. 7:9-12; Rom. 7:12).

THE LAW'S PURPOSE

When we read of the Law's purpose in Scripture, there appears to be nothing that would render it inappropriate for our day. Indeed, there is everything to commend it to the modern Christian.

1. The Law defines sin. What the Christian is called to restrain and resist in the world is sin. The Law is essential to our struggle against evil in that it defines sin. "Whoever committeth sin transgresseth also the law: for sin is the transgression of the law" (1 John 3:4, KJV). "For until the law sin was in the world, but sin is not imputed when there is no law" (Rom. 5:13). "On the contrary, I would not have known sin except through the law. For I would not have known covetousness unless the law had said, 'You shall not covet'" (Rom. 7:7b). Other references speak of "lawlessness" as reprehensible and worthy of God's judgment.[3]

2. The Law convicts of sin. With the preaching of the Law there follows the conviction of sin, in that Law expressly prohibits and judges sin. By pointing out sin, the Law stirs the heart, bringing a knowledge of the death-dealing consequence of lawless behavior.

17

What shall we say then? Is the law sin? Certainly not! On the contrary, I would not have known sin except through the law. For I would not have known covetousness unless the law had said, "You shall not covet." . . . I was alive once without the law, but when the commandment came, sin revived and I died. . . . For sin, taking occasion by the commandment, deceived me, and by it killed me. (Rom. 7:7, 9, 11; cp. James 2:9)

3. The Law condemns transgression. The Law also carries with it the penalty of its infraction, clearly showing the destructive consequences of lawless conduct. "The law brings about wrath; for where there is no law there is no transgression" (Rom. 4:15). "For whoever shall keep the whole law, and yet stumble in one point, he is guilty of all" (James 2:10). "For as many as are of the works of the law are under the curse; for it is written, 'Cursed is everyone who does not continue in all things which are written in the book of the law, to do them'" (Gal. 3:10; see also Deut. 11:26, 28).

4. The Law drives people to Christ. In that the Law severely judges sin, leaving men exposed to the wrath of God; and in that the Law cannot save, it drives them to Christ. "And the commandment, which was to bring life, I found to bring death" (Rom. 7:10). "Therefore the law was our tutor to bring us to Christ, that we might be justified by faith" (Gal. 3:24). The theonomic ethic does not hold that Law-keeping has ever or will ever merit salvation for anyone. In fact, it causes them to despair of their own righteousness so that they might seek the righteousness of another: Christ the Lord.

5. The Law restrains evil. When the Law is properly understood and its breach feared, it tends to exercise a restraining power within over the souls of men. When enacted in the public sphere, it reduces criminal activity by threatening judgment. For instance, when "thou shalt not kill" is backed up by the sanction, "He who strikes a man so that he dies shall surely be put to death" (Ex. 21:12), the cost of crime becomes prohibitive.

This is as God designed it to be.

> But we know that the law is good if one uses it lawfully, knowing this: that the law is not made for a righteous person, but for the lawless and insubordinate, for the ungodly and for sinners, for the unholy and profane, for murderers of fathers and murderers of mothers, for manslayers, for fornicators, for sodomites, for kidnappers, for liars, for perjurers, and if there is any other thing that is contrary to sound doctrine, according to the glorious gospel of the blessed God which was committed to my trust. (1 Tim 1:8-11; cp. Ps. 119:11)

6. The Law guides sanctification. The Law does not have the power to sanctify; that is the ministry of the Holy Spirit as He operates in the gospel. But the Law sets forth the God-ordained *pattern of righteous behavior* and therefore provides an *objective standard* for the Spirit-filled Christian so that he might know what God expects of him.

> For what the law could not do in that it was weak through the flesh, God did by sending His own Son in the likeness of sinful flesh, on account of sin: He con-

demned sin in the flesh, that the righteous requirement of the law might be fulfilled in us who do not walk according to the flesh but according to the Spirit. (Rom. 8:3-4).

"To those who are without law, [I am] as without law (*not being without law toward God, but under law toward Christ*), that I might win those who are without law" (1 Cor. 9:21, emphasis added; see also Lev. 20:8; Ps. 119:105; Prov. 6:23).

NOTES

1. See note 5 in the introduction.
2. Matt. 26:28; Mark 14:24; Luke 22:20; 1 Cor. 11:25; 2 Cor. 3:7ff.; Heb. 8:6ff.
3. Matt. 7:23; 13:41; 23:28; 24:12; Acts 8:23; Rom. 3:20; 6:19; 1 Cor. 13:6; Titus 2:14; Heb. 1:9; James 3:6. The King James Version rendering "iniquity" is literally "lawlessness" in the Greek: *a* ("no") and *nomos* ("law").

CHAPTER
THREE

THE LORD JESUS CHRIST
AND GOD'S LAW

The central personage of prophecy and gospel is the Lord Jesus Christ. There are several respects in which we may see that the He intended His new covenant people to keep the Law of God. In no way did He undercut the validity of the Law when He came. In fact, He confirmed it.

CHRIST EXPRESSLY AFFIRMED THE LAW

That truth is most clearly taught in Matthew 5:16-20.

[16] Let your light so shine before men, that they may see your good works and glorify your Father in

heaven. [17] Do not think that I came to destroy the Law or the Prophets. I did not come to destroy but to fulfill. [18] For assuredly, I say to you, till heaven and earth pass away, one jot or one tittle will by no means pass from the law till all is fulfilled. [19] Whoever therefore breaks one of the least of these commandments, and teaches men so, shall be called least in the kingdom of heaven; but whoever does and teaches them, he shall be called great in the kingdom of heaven. [20] For I say to you, that unless your righteousness exceeds the righteousness of the scribes and Pharisees, you will by no means enter the kingdom of heaven.

In the following pages I will give a brief, running commentary on points of the passages of exegetical significance to the theonomic position.[1] The reader is urged to keep his Bible open to the passage for consultation as these exegetical remarks are provided.

Immediately after urging His hearers to God-glorifying works, Christ says, "do not think that I came to destroy the Law or the Prophets" (v. 17). He begins defining the character of those works in terms of God's Law. The phrase "do not think" is an ingressive aorist verb that means, "do not begin to think." He does not want the thought He is about to mention even to cross the minds of His hearers. He does not want to be misunderstood as He corrects distortions and abuses of the Law of God He encounters during His ministry.

When he says, "do not think that I came to *destroy* the Law or the Prophets" (v. 17), he uses a Greek word that means to "dismantle, abrogate, dispose of thoroughly." Rather than allowing His hearers even to begin to think this, He says, "I have not come to destroy, *but* to fulfill" (v. 17). The conjunction "but" here is the strong adversative (Gk.: *alla*). It provides sharp contrast, as in Matthew 10:34, which exactly parallels Matthew 5:17 in form and structure. Matthew 10:34 reads: "Do not think that I came to bring peace on earth. I did not come to bring peace but a sword." Notice the strong contrast between "peace" and a "sword." Likewise in Matthew 5:17 Jesus contrasts destroying the Law with fulfilling it; the ideas are juxtaposed as *opposites*.

The word "fulfill" (v. 17), which the Lord uses here, cannot imply "to live out and complete it, so as to do away with it," or anything similar. Since the word is contrasted with "destroy," it would be wrongly interpreted as "fulfill and do away with." The abrogation of the Law is the very thing Christ denies. "Fulfill" here may mean one of two things.

(1) It may mean "to confirm, establish." Romans 3:31 (which uses a different verb) says: "Do we then make void the law through faith? Certainly not! On the contrary, we establish the law." Confirmation of the Law is certainly a New Testament concept, according to Paul. (2) Or it may mean "fill up to full measure." This would indicate restoring it to its true meaning, in opposition to Pharisaic distortions.

Matthew 5:20 in the context here strongly suggests the latter interpretation (although it does not exclude the former—indeed, it implies it): "For I say to you, that unless your righteousness exceeds the righteousness of the scribes and Pharisees, you will by no means enter the kingdom of heaven" (cp. Matt. 15:3-9; 23:23). The scribes and Pharisees had so redefined the Law in terms of their own system of thought, they had virtually emptied it of its true meaning. Christ came to restore the Law to the original, divine intention.

The word "for" (v. 18) introduces an explanation of verse 17. What follows the word gives justification for what precedes.

When Christ says "assuredly" (or "verily" in the KJV) (v. 18), He emphasizes the importance of the following statement. The Lord often uses this word to draw His hearers' attention to an important observation He is about to make. That observation follows. "For assuredly, I say to you, till heaven and earth pass away, one jot or one tittle will by no means pass from the law till all is fulfilled" (Matt. 5:18). The reference "heaven and earth pass away" (v. 18) indicates a comparison between the stability of the Law and that of the world (cp. Eccl. 1:4). The Law cannot be disannulled until the material heavens and earth pass away (and even then "till" does not require that it will pass away at that time).

The phrase "jot or tittle" (v. 18) makes reference to the smallest Hebrew letter (the *yodh*, or "jot") and the ornamental strokes on the letters ("tittles"). Christ is concerned to show that God's Law in its totality is protected by God's authority. His repetition of "one" before both "jot" and "tittle" (v. 18) is important. In Hebrew thought, repetition is commonly used for strong emphasis.

"Till all is fulfilled" (v. 18) may literally be translated, "Until all things be accomplished." Thus, this statement parallels "till heaven and earth pass away." In other words, not the smallest letter or stroke of the law will pass away before history ends.[2]

He then backs up and reinforces what He has just stated: "Whoever therefore breaks one of the least of these commandments, and teaches men so, shall be called least in the kingdom of heaven; but whoever does and teaches them, he shall be called great in the kingdom of heaven" (Matt. 5:19). "Least commandment" (v. 19) repeats the emphasis of the small aspects of the Law in order to show its binding significance. If the least things are so important, how much more the large aspects of the Law?

The one who goes against His teaching in this regard is considered "least in the kingdom of heaven" (v. 19). This speaks of that person's status in the kingdom Christ established on earth.[3] It involves the post-Old Testament, post-John the Baptist era (Mark 11:13ff.; Luke 16:16ff.), which so many of His parables dealt with (e.g., Matt. 13).

Following this strong statement of the Law's validity, Christ rebuts scribal distortions of the Law by their adherence to oral interpretation, rather than a faithful obedience to the written law (Matt. 5:21ff.). Notice two things: (1) The contrasts drawn are between what is "written" and what is "said of old" (by the rabbis). When the Lord refers to God's Law in its true, undistorted sense, He always says, "It is written" (e.g., Matt. 4:4, 6, 7, 10). (2) He has just made a strong statement as to the Law's continuing validity. Consistency would require that Matthew 5:21ff. not allow an undermining of His teaching.

27

CHRIST EMPHATICALLY TAUGHT THE LAW'S RELEVANCE

The Lord rebukes the Pharisees, for instance, not for their keeping the small tithe obligations of the Law, but for their doing so *while overlooking the weightier matters of the Law.* "Woe to you, scribes and Pharisees, hypocrites! For you pay tithe of mint and anise and cumin, and have neglected the weightier matters of the law: justice and mercy and faith. These you ought to have done, without leaving the others undone" (Matt. 23:23). They constantly made void God's Law through their traditions (Mark 7:1-13).

Jesus teaches that the Law is the Golden Rule of service to God and man. "Therefore, whatever you want men to do to you, do also to them, for this is the Law and the Prophets" (Matt. 7:12).

He teaches that love is defined by Law. The Jewish lawyer asked Him:

> "Teacher, which is the great commandment in the law?" Jesus said to him, "'You shall love the LORD your God with all your heart, with all your soul, and with all your mind.' This is the first and great commandment. And the second is like it: 'You shall love your neighbor as yourself.' On these two commandments hang all the Law and the Prophets." (Matt. 22:36-40)

Love is not feeling or nondescript action. It is obedient action defined by the strictures of God-ordained Law.

CHRIST UPHELD THE LAW'S CIVIL FUNCTION

Even one of the laws most commonly misunderstood and misused today against the theonomic view is upheld by Christ. That is the law calling for capital punishment for incorrigible crimes. Even the parents of a dangerous person are to turn him over to civil authorities for his capital punishment.

> But He answered and said to them, "Why do you also transgress the commandment of God because of your tradition? For God commanded, saying, 'Honor your father and your mother'; and, 'He who curses father or mother, let him be put to death.' But you say, 'Whoever says to his father or mother, "Whatever profit you might have received from me has been dedicated to the temple"—is released from honoring his father or mother.' Thus you have made the commandment of God of no effect by your tradition." (Matt. 15:3-6)

Christ rebukes the Pharisees for circumventing this law. (Remember His warning in Matt. 5:19-20! Our righteousness should exceed that of the scribes and Pharisees.)

This law has to do with a son old enough to be a threat to the community through criminal activity. He is described variously as a glutton and drunkard, a stubborn and rebellious son who will not heed or obey his parents (Deut. 21:18-20) and is a physical threat to them (Ex. 21:15). This is not a ten-year-old who refuses to take out the garbage. The son in question has become an enemy and a curse to his parents.

Whatever we might initially think of this law, we must remember that it was ordained by the Lord God.

29

This should forestall the Christian's mockery of it, giving him pause to consider its true significance.

CHRIST PERFECTLY KEPT THE LAW

The Scripture teaches that Jesus came to keep the Law. "Then I said, 'Behold, I come; In the scroll of the Book it is written of me. I delight to do Your will, O my God, And Your law is within my heart'" (Ps. 40:7-8). In fact, He was born under the Law (Gal. 4:4). Thus He kept the Law in detail in His personal life (Matt. 8:4; 17:24; Mark 11:16-17).

Because of the nature of sin as transgression of the Law,[4] Christ was sinless because He kept the Law fully. Thus, he could say, "Which of you convicts Me of sin?" (John 8:46; cp. 1 John 3:4; John 15:10). This being the case, He is our perfect example of Law-keeping.

> He who says, "I know Him," and does not keep His commandments, is a liar, and the truth is not in him. But whoever keeps His word, truly the love of God is perfected in him. By this we know that we are in Him. He who says he abides in Him ought himself also to walk just as He walked." (1 John 2:4-6)

Following after Christ and keeping His commandments are synonymous, according to John.

CHRIST SAVED US IN TERMS OF THE LAW

The Lord died in terms of the Law for us. He came "to redeem those who were under the law, that we might receive the adoption as sons" (Gal. 4:5; cp. Col. 2:14; Heb. 9:22). In fact, His death eternally accented the need for and the validity of the Law. The Law could not be set aside, even to spare Christ. "He who did not spare His own Son, but delivered Him up for us all, how shall He not with Him also freely give us all things?" (Rom. 8:32; cp. Heb. 9:22-26). Faith, then, confirms the Law's validity (Rom. 3:31). If the Law could not be set aside to spare God's own Son, how may we surmise that it will be set aside for the New Covenant era? It is the standard of God's righteousness, the breach of which brings condemnation. The Cross is an eternal testimony to the righteousness of and the continuing validity of God's Law.

NOTES

1. More detailed consideration of the passages can be found in Greg L. Bahnsen, *Theonomy in Christian Ethics*, 2d ed. (Phillipsburg, N.J.: Presbyterian and Reformed, 1984).
2. See chapter 5 for a discussion of the ceremonial and sacrificial laws. These are prophetic laws that prefigure the coming of Christ and symbolize redemption. For that reason they no longer bind the new covenant era Christian.
3. Matt. 3:2; 4:17; 10:7; 11:11-12.
4. See earlier presentation above.

CHAPTER
FOUR

THE NEW TESTAMENT
AND GOD'S LAW

The unity of Scripture assumes the continuance of God's Law. God's Word reveals to us a unified and righteous ethic. "The Scripture cannot be broken" (John 10:35b). "All Scripture is given by inspiration of God, and is profitable for doctrine, for reproof, for correction, for instruction in righteousness, that the man of God may be complete, thoroughly equipped for every good work" (2 Tim. 3:16-17). The Christian's manual for holy living is *all* Scripture."

All Scripture, not just the New Testament, is given that the Christian might be "complete" and "thoroughly equipped for every good work." Interestingly, 2 Timothy is the last book written by Paul and is probably the last book written in the New Testament.[1]

The New Testament Expressly Confirms the Law

One of the most noble of Christian virtues is faith. It is the God-ordained instrument of justification. God's gracious provision of salvation on the basis of grace and through the means of faith is often thought to abrogate the Law of God for today. Yet Paul, the great Apostle of Faith, tells us that faith confirms the Law. "Do we then make void the law through faith? Certainly not! On the contrary, we establish the law" (Rom. 3:31).

Paul, who is known in the New Testament as the apostle to the Gentiles and to the uncircumcised (Rom. 15:16; Gal. 2:9; Eph. 3:8), nevertheless, upheld the "Jewish" Mosaic Law as an ethical ideal for God's people. When he wrote to the church at Rome, he wrote to a gentile church (Rom. 1:13; 15:12; 16:4). "Therefore the law is holy, and the commandment holy and just and good. . . . For we know that the law is spiritual" (Rom. 7:12, 14). And this was well into the new covenant era.

New Testament Teachers Use the Law in Teaching

1. Christ based His teaching on the Law. Christ was not hesitant to base His teaching solidly on the Old Testament Scriptures, including the moral obligations of the Law. "He said to him, 'What is written in the law? What is your reading of it?'" (Luke 10:26). We should recall Matthew 7:12, also: "Therefore, whatever you want men to do to you, do also to them, for this is the

Law and the Prophets" (see also Matt. 12:5; 19:4; Luke 10:26; 16:17, 29-30; John 8:17).

2. *Even detail case laws are cited as binding directives.* The apostles were not fearful of citing Old Testament case laws, despite the abuses of Judaizers (see Acts 15; Gal. 2). In 1 Timothy 5:18 Paul cites Deuteronomy 25:4 to confirm an obligation upon the church. "Let the elders who rule well be counted worthy of double honor, especially those who labor in the word and doctrine. For the Scripture says, 'You shall not muzzle an ox while it treads out the grain,' and, 'The laborer is worthy of his wages'" (1 Tim. 5:17-18; cp. also 2 Cor. 6:14 and Deut. 22:10; Rom. 10:6-8 and Deut. 30:11-13; Acts 23:1-5 and Ex. 22:28; Lev. 19:15; Deut. 25:2).

CHRISTIAN CONDUCT IS BASED ON LAW OBEDIENCE

1. *Love is given definition by the Law.* Following the example of Christ already noted above, the apostles define love in terms of law. And love is the greatest of Christian virtues (1 Cor. 13:13). "Love does no harm to a neighbor; therefore love is the fulfillment of the law" (Rom. 13:10; see also Matt. 22:36-40; Gal. 5:14).

2. *Keeping God's commandments is important.* Paul clearly teaches the importance of "keeping the commandments of God," when he writes, "Circumcision is nothing and uncircumcision is nothing, but keeping the commandments of God is what matters" (1 Cor. 7:19). That is why he writes in a later chapter, "Let your women keep silent in the churches, for they are not

permitted to speak; but they are to be submissive, as the law also says" (1 Cor. 14:34). John agrees with Paul. "Now by this we know that we know Him, if we keep His commandments. He who says, 'I know Him,' and does not keep His commandments, is a liar, and the truth is not in him" (1 John 2:3-4; cf. 5:3).

GOSPEL PREACHING DEPENDS ON GOD'S LAW

The Law convicts of sin, as we have shown before (1 John 3:4; Matt. 19:16-24; John 7:19; Acts 7:53; James 2:9). Without the conviction of sin there will be no turning to the Savior in repentance for salvation. Without the call to repentance there is no preaching of the gospel of Jesus Christ.

Moreover, God's judgment of sinners will be based on the Law. "And then I will declare to them, 'I never knew you; depart from Me, you who practice lawlessness!'" (Matt. 7:23; cf. 13:41; Rom. 2:12-15; James 2:10-12). Men will be judged on the basis of an objective standard: God's Law. Such a judgment will determine the degree of punishment that a person receives in hell (cp. Luke 12:47; Rev. 20:12).

NOTES

1. Contrary to popular opinion, Revelation was not the last book written. See Kenneth L. Gentry, Jr., *Before Jerusalem Fell: Dating the Book of Revelation* (Tyler, Tex.: Institute for Christian Economics, 1989).

CHAPTER
FIVE

ALLEGED NEGATIVE PASSAGES

Despite there being such a strong case for the theonomic ethic in Scripture, certain passages are often brought forward as contrary evidence. These negative passages must be reviewed in light of three factors:

1. The foundation of theonomic ethics is well established scripturally (e.g., Matt. 5:17-19; Rom. 3:31). There is too much positive evidence available to proof-text God's Law away. The Scripture is noncontradictory. Any apparent contradictions must be interpreted in light of Scripture's infallibility.

2. Much of the historical background of the New Testament is the struggle of Christianity with Jewish pride. "Is He the God of the Jews only? Is He not also the God of the Gentiles? Yes, of the Gentiles also" (Rom. 3:29).[1] This debate can be misconstrued as contra-God's Law if not kept in the proper perspective. We are so far

removed from the Jew-Christian debate today that we may overlook its significance in the early church.

3. The historical background in other instances is clearly legalism: ". . . knowing that a man is not justified by the works of the law but by faith in Jesus Christ, even we have believed in Christ Jesus, that we might be justified by faith in Christ and not by the works of the law; for by the works of the law no flesh shall be justified" (Gal. 2:16).[2] No proper understanding of God's Law can be legalistic. That is, no truly evangelical understanding of the function of God's Law can allow Law-keeping as a basis for salvation, which is what legalism teaches.

A SURVEY OF PASSAGES

Passages that appear to negate the theonomic use of the Law of God today tend to fall into four classes:

- Class 1: Those which renounce the Law as a means of justification (see above).
- Class 2: Passages emphasizing the death-dealing nature of sin as it relates to the Law.
- Class 3: Those pertaining to the transient ceremonial aspects of the Law.
- Class 4: Passages that are simply misinterpreted altogether.

ROMANS 6:14

Romans 6:14 is the most famous antitheonomic passage. "For sin shall not have dominion over you, for you are not under law but under grace." It is a Class 4 passage. Notice two things:

1. Paul is not referring to the Mosaic Law , but to a law-principle for salvation, i.e., legalism. God's Law is not an enemy of God's grace, for God's Law endorses the grace of God.[3]

2. The phrase "under law" means being a slave to legalism. According to the context, we are to be "slaves to righteousness" because we are "under grace."

> Do you not know that to whom you present yourselves slaves to obey, you are that one's slaves whom you obey, whether of sin to death, or of obedience to righteousness? But God be thanked that though you were slaves of sin, yet you obeyed from the heart that form of doctrine to which you were delivered. And having been set free from sin, you became slaves of righteousness. (Rom. 6:16-18)

ROMANS 7:4

Romans 7:4 is a Class 2 passage. "Therefore, my brethren, you also have become dead to the law through the body of Christ, that you may be married to another, even to Him who was raised from the dead, that we should bear fruit to God."

To properly understand this verse, we should note that it is the *believer* who has died, *not the Law*. That is a rather big difference! The Law requires perfection and holds us back from God as we fail because of its righteous demands. But in Christ, we died to the Law *as a condemner*. We have not died to that which Paul, in the

43

same epistle, says faith establishes (Rom. 3:31), sanctification needs (Rom. 7:12, 14), and the Holy Spirit
prompts (Rom. 8:3-4).

ROMANS 10:4

Romans 10:4 is clearly a Class 1 passage. "For
Christ is the end of the law for righteousness to everyone who believes." Here Paul simply says, contrary to
Pharisaic Judaism, that Christ is the end of the Law for
righteousness, or justification before God. No one can
be justified before God by adhering to God's Law, however meticulously.

2 CORINTHIANS 3

2 Corinthians 3 is a Class 4 passage. The Law is
considered in its death-dealing sense because men
break it. God "also made us sufficient as ministers of
the new covenant, not of the letter but of the Spirit; for
the letter kills, but the Spirit gives life" (2 Cor. 3:6-8).

Paul notes that the new covenant outshines the old
covenant in glory because it has the power to enliven
and impart life.

> But if the ministry of death, written and engraved on
> stones, was glorious, so that the children of Israel could
> not look steadily at the face of Moses because of the
> glory of his countenance, which glory was passing
> away, how will the ministry of the Spirit not be more
> glorious? For if the ministry of condemnation had glory,
> the ministry of righteousness exceeds much more in
> glory. (2 Cor. 3:7b-9)

It was the *glory* of the old covenant order that faded, not the Law:

> For if what is passing away was glorious, what remains is much more glorious. Therefore, since we have such hope, we use great boldness of speech—unlike Moses, who put a veil over his face so that the children of Israel could not look steadily at the end of what was passing away." (2 Cor. 3:11-13)

GALATIANS

In Galatians we have passages that may be designated Classes 1 and 3. The Galatians were trying to keep the ceremonial aspects of the Law in hopes of gaining justification before God (Gal. 5:1-4; 2:19, 21; 3:11). But Christ has delivered us from the curse that the broken Law demands. "Christ has redeemed us from the curse of the law, having become a curse for us (for it is written, 'Cursed is everyone who hangs on a tree')" (Gal. 3:13). The Law itself is not a "curse," but it contains a curse for those who break it.

JOHN 1:17

John 1:17 is a Class 4 passage. "For the law was given through Moses, but grace and truth came through Jesus Christ." The contrast here is not between Law and grace or truth, but between Moses and Christ in their roles in the unfolding of divine revelation: The Law was *through Moses* (it was not his own). Grace and truth were actually *realized* in Christ (it was His own). Thus, the Law indirectly manifests God as a reflection,

45

whereas Christ directly manifests God as the "exact representation" (John 1:14, 18; Heb. 1:3).

LUKE 16:16

Luke 16:16 is a Class 4 passage. "The law and the prophets were until John. Since that time the kingdom of God has been preached, and everyone is pressing into it." It merely teaches that the age of the Law and prophets historically led up to the coming of Christ. Nothing here is contra-theonomic.

THE CEREMONIAL LAW

The ceremonial law is often brought forward to undermine a proper exposition of Matthew 5:17-19, as given in an earlier chapter. However, we must recognize, first, that God's Law reflects two sorts of truth: moral and restorative. That is, the Law reflects God's holy justice and His gracious salvation. The ceremonial law, *by design*, was never intended to be an end in itself. It always prophetically and typically looked forward to the coming Redeemer. It foreshadowed the eternal truths of Christ's work and it was intended to be superseded.

> Therefore, if perfection were through the Levitical priesthood (for under it the people received the law), what further need was there that another priest should rise according to the order of Melchizedek, and not be called according to the order of Aaron? For the priesthood being changed, of necessity there is also a change of the law. (Heb. 7:11, 12)

46

Second, Christ's coming confirmed the essential meaning of the ceremonies and eternally validated their teaching. Christ is the reality of which they were but the shadow.

Third, we have the ceremonies observed for us in Christ. He did not destroy their meaning, but transformed the way they are to be kept. *He* is our sacrifice (1 Cor. 5:7; 1 Pet. 1:19; John 1:29). Sometimes we may find it difficult to determine what laws are ceremonial and what ones are not, but this does not destroy the principle of theonomic ethics.

NOTES

1. See also 1:13; 2:17-20, 28-29; 9:31; 10:3.
2. Cp. Gal. 2:21-3:3, 10, 11; 5:4.
3. Ex. 32:13; 33:13; Jer. 3:12; 1 Kings 8:46, 48-53; Heb. 1:1ff.

CHAPTER
SIX

THE WORLD-SCOPE
OF GOD'S LAW

It is often argued that the Mosaic Law was expressly designed for use only in old covenant Israel. Its relevance was exclusively for the special redemptive nation in pre-Christian times.

Dispensationalists are prone to use this argument quite vigorously: "The stipulations of Sinai were not for the nations in general but to a people under grace. . . . Since nations around Israel were not called to adopt the Mosaic Covenant, it seems evident that the pagan nations would not be judged by the law of Moses."[1]

THEONOMIC ETHICS AND THE NATIONS

The following are a few responses to that sort of objection:

1. The dispensationalist objection confuses moral commandments and covenantal form. The moral commands are distinguishable from the covenantal system in which they are found. For example, in both the new covenant and the old, we are commanded to love father and mother (cp. Deut. 5:16 and Eph. 6:2). This does not mean that the old covenant and the new covenant are the same!

The old covenant form, which included the sacrificial system and other ceremonial requirements and was established only with Israel, encoded numerous divinely ordained moral requirements, which are the perpetually obligatory commandments of God. Unchanging moral requirements may be distinguished from the changing historical and redemptive trappings in which they are found. Moral commandments (justice defining) are distinguishable from distinctive ceremonial laws (redemption expounding), as is evidenced in the Old Testament itself. God contrasts the moral and ceremonial, when He says, "For I desire mercy and not sacrifice, And the knowledge of God more than burnt offerings" (Hos. 6:6).

Elsewhere we witness the same. "Then Samuel said: 'Has the LORD as great delight in burnt offerings and sacrifices, As in obeying the voice of the LORD? Behold, to obey is better than sacrifice, And to heed than the fat of rams'" (1 Sam. 15:22). David writes:

> Deliver me from bloodguiltiness, O God, The God of my salvation, And my tongue shall sing aloud of Your righteousness. O Lord, open my lips, And my mouth shall show forth Your praise. For You do not desire sac-

rifice, or else I would give it; You do not delight in burnt offering. The sacrifices of God are a broken spirit, A broken and a contrite heart—These, O God, You will not despise. (Ps. 51:14-17)[2]

2. *God's Law was in fact designed to be a model for the nations.*

Therefore be careful to observe them; for this is your wisdom and your understanding in the sight of the peoples who will hear all these statutes, and say, "Surely this great nation is a wise and understanding people." For what great nation is there that has God so near to it, as the LORD our God is to us, for whatever reason we may call upon Him? And what great nation is there that has such statutes and righteous judgments as are in all this law which I set before you this day? (Deut. 4:6-8)

This is indicated elsewhere, as well, including 1 Kings 10:1, 8-9; Isaiah 24:5; 51:4; Psalms 2:9ff.; 47:1-2; 94:10-12; 97:1-2; 119:46, 118-119; Proverbs 16:12; Ecclesiastes 12:13. God does not have a double standard of justice (cf. Deut. 25:13-16; Lev. 19:35-37).

3. *The nations around Israel were often judged for breaching God's moral standards, but never for breaching the Mosaic covenantal form.* Israel is warned, while preparing to enter the Land:

Do not defile yourselves with any of these things; for by all these the nations are defiled, which I am casting out before you. For the land is defiled; therefore I visit the punishment of its iniquity upon it, and the land vomits out its inhabitants. You shall therefore keep My statutes and My judgments, and shall not commit any of these abominations, either any of your own nation or any stranger who sojourns among you (for all these abominations the men of the land have done, who were before you, and thus the land is defiled). (Lev. 18:24-27)[3]

The same truth may be seen earlier in Abraham's day in the judgment of Sodom and Gomorrah (Gen. 19:15; cp. 2 Pet. 2:9).

4. *Church and state were separate in the Old Testament era.* Dispensationalists accuse theonomists of promoting the "fusion of church and state"[4] or intermingling the two institutions.[5] Such a merging, they argue, was appropriate to Israel's particular place in redemptive history, but not to nations outside of Israel. What they fail to realize is that theonomists do not argue for any such union of church and state. There was no such union in Israel itself. Although there was a close relation between church and state, they remained separate institutions. There was a distinction between the civil ruler, Moses, and the priestly head, Aaron; between the offices of priest and king; between the temple and palace (1 Sam. 13:11; 2 Chron. 19:5-11; 26:16-21). To argue for the normativity of God's Law today is not to deny the validity of those distinctions.

5. *People from all nations are under obligation to God's Law today.* Paul's writings are very clear in this regard: ". . . who, knowing the righteous judgment of God, that those who practice such things are worthy of death, not only do the same but also approve of those who prac-

tice them" (Rom 1:32). Here Paul is not limiting God's judgment to any one sin, but he speaks of the complex of sinfulness depicted in the preceding verses.[6] A few verses later he writes:

> For as many as have sinned without law will also perish without law, and as many as have sinned in the law will be judged by the law (for not the hearers of the law are just in the sight of God, but the doers of the law will be justified; for when Gentiles, who do not have the law, by nature do the things contained in the law, these, although not having the law, are a law to themselves, who show the work of the law written in their hearts, their conscience also bearing witness, and between themselves their thoughts accusing or else excusing them). (Rom. 2:12-15)

A very clear statement by Paul is found in Romans 3:19. "Now we know that whatever the law says, it says to those who are under the law, that every mouth may be stopped, and all the world may become guilty before God" (cf. 12:19-13:10; 1 Tim. 1:8).

All of this is expected in light of the coming of the Messiah, who will teach the nations God's Law.

> Now it shall come to pass in the latter days That the mountain of the Lord's house Shall be established on the top of the mountains, and shall be exalted above the hills; And all nations shall flow to it. Many people shall come and say, "Come, and let us go up to the mountain of the LORD, To the house of the God of Jacob; He will teach us His ways, And we shall walk in His paths." For out of Zion shall go forth the law, And the word of the LORD from Jerusalem. (Isa. 2:2-3)

Thus, as noted earlier, God's Law in our era is considered to be "just" (Rom. 7:12; Heb. 2:2) and "good" (Rom. 7:12; 1 Tim. 1:8).

NOTES

1. H. Wayne House and Thomas D. Ice, *Dominion Theology: Blessing or Curse?* (Portland, Oreg.: Multnomah, 1988), pp. 128, 129.
2. See also Prov. 21:3; Isa. 1:10-17.
3. See also Deut. 7:5-6, 16, 25; 12:1-4; 19:29-32; Amos 1:6 (Ex. 21:16; Deut. 24:7); Nah. 3:4 (Ex. 22:18; Lev. 19:21); Hab. 2:6 (Ex. 22:25-27; Deut. 24:6, 10-13); Hab. 2:12 (cp. Mic. 3:10).
4. House and Ice, *Dominion Theology*, p. 95.
5. Ibid., p. 339.
6. For a fuller discussion of Rom. 1:32, see Kenneth L. Gentry, "Civil Sanctions in the New Testament," Gary North, ed., *Theonomy: An Informed Response* (Tyler, Tex.: Institute for Christian Economics, 1991).

CHAPTER
SEVEN

THE PRACTICAL BENEFITS
OF THEONOMIC ETHICS

By way of illustrating the practicality of the Law of God (which has been set forth as a moral obligation heretofore), I will briefly list a few of the benefits built into theonomic ethics.

SCRIPTURAL BENEFITS

One of the most immediate benefits of theonomy is that we are left with an intact Word of God. The theonomic ethic does not approach Scripture with the presupposition that certain parts of the Old Testament must be cast aside unless repeated in the New Testament. Rather, *only a word from God in Scripture itself is allowed to set aside any portion of Scripture.*

For instance, the Book of Hebrews clearly sets aside the sacrificial system, its purpose of pointing to Christ having been accomplished. For the adherent to the theonomic ethic, the Bible is left intact as a unified Word from God that has relevance for all time.

PUBLIC BENEFITS

GENERAL BENEFITS

1. In the self-consciously Christian approach to social ethics, an unchanging Law becomes the basis of social order, rather than the changing whims of legislators, the mood of the populace, or the fads of revolutionaries. God's Law is unchangingly righteous. "Whatever I command you, be careful to observe it; you shall not add to it nor take away from it" (Deut. 12:32).[1]

All law is necessarily religious, for all law is an expression of morality. And morality is based on ideas of ultimacy and value. By their very nature ultimacy and values are religious conceptions. The Christian religion, being the truth (as demonstrated by a proper apologetic), provides an inerrant and authoritative Word of unchanging righteousness as the standard of social morality.

2. National prosperity abounds in terms only of God-defined righteousness, because we live in a moral universe (Prov. 15:3). "Righteousness exalts a nation, but sin is a reproach to any people" (Prov. 14:34). God

is sovereign in His providential administration of the affairs of the world. Consequently, the prophets can poetically portray the clouds as the dust of His feet (Nah. 1:3-6). Job can speak of God as directing the lightning (Job 37:3). He even controls the number of hairs on our heads and the life and death of sparrows (Matt. 10:29-30). Indeed, He "works all things according to the counsel of His will" (Eph. 1:11). History has meaning and purpose by His personal involvement. He has ordained that, culturally, Law obedience determines national destinies in the long run (Deut. 28).

SOCIETAL BENEFITS

Many societal benefits accrue from a theonomic approach to law and order. Here are a few examples.

1. It obligates government to maintain just monetary policies.

> You shall not have in your bag differing weights, a heavy and a light. You shall not have in your house differing measures, a large and a small. You shall have a perfect and just weight, a perfect and just measure, that your days may be lengthened in the land which the LORD your God is giving you. (Deut. 25:13-15[2])

God's Law thereby prohibits three contemporary monetary phenomena that have contributed so heavily to the economically precarious position of modern nations: fiat money, fractional reserve banking, and deficit spending.

2. It provides a moral basis for elective governmental officials.

"Choose wise, understanding, and knowledgeable men from among your tribes, and I will make them heads over you.". . . So I took the heads of your tribes, wise and knowledgeable men, and made them heads over you, leaders of thousands, leaders of hundreds, leaders of fifties, leaders of tens, and officers for your tribes. . . . "You shall not show partiality in judgment; you shall hear the small as well as the great; you shall not be afraid in any man's presence, for the judgment is God's. The case that is too hard for you, bring it to me, and I will hear it." (Deut. 1:13, 15, 17)

3. It forbids undue, abusive taxation of the rich. "The rich shall not give more and the poor shall not give less than half a shekel, when you give an offering to the LORD, to make atonement for yourselves" (Ex. 30:15). Communism punishes the wealthy—and the poor, as the former Soviet Union clearly demonstrated. God's Law protects the rights of both the poor and the rich.

4. It calls for the abolishing of the prison system and establishing a system of just restitution.

"If a man steals an ox or a sheep, and slaughters it or sells it, he shall restore five oxen for an ox and four sheep for a sheep. If the thief is found breaking in, and he is struck so that he dies, there shall be no guilt for his bloodshed. If the sun has risen on him, there shall be guilt for his bloodshed. He should make full restitution; if he has nothing, then he shall be sold for his theft.[3] If the theft is certainly found alive in his hand, whether it is an ox or donkey or sheep, he shall restore double." (Ex. 22:1-4[4])

A system of just restitution would eliminate taxpayer support of criminals, rid society of a major breed-

ing and training ground for criminals, and justly reim-
burse crime victims.

5. A theonomic approach also forbids the release,
pardoning, and paroling of murderers by requiring their
execution.

> But if anyone hates his neighbor, lies in wait for him,
> rises against him and strikes him mortally, so that he
> dies, and he flees to one of these cities, then the elders
> of his city shall send and bring him from there, and de-
> liver him over to the hand of the avenger of blood, that
> he may die. Your eye shall not pity him, but you shall
> put away the guilt of innocent blood from Israel, that it
> may go well with you. (Deut. 19:11-13)

6. It prohibits industrial pollution that destroys the
value of property. "If fire breaks out and catches in
thorns, so that stacked grain, standing grain, or the field
is consumed, he who kindled the fire shall surely make
restitution" (Ex. 22:6).

7. It punishes malicious, frivolous malpractice
suits.

> If a false witness rises against any man to testify against
> him of wrongdoing, then both men in the controversy
> shall stand before the LORD, before the priests and the
> judges who serve in those days. And the judges shall
> make diligent inquiry, and indeed, if the witness is a
> false witness, who has testified falsely against his
> brother, then you shall do to him as he thought to have
> done to his brother; so you shall put away the evil per-
> son from among you. And those who remain shall hear
> and fear, and hereafter they shall not again commit such
> evil among you. Your eye shall not pity; but life shall

be for life, eye for eye, tooth for tooth, hand for hand, foot for foot. (Deut. 19:16-21)

8. It forbids abortion rights.

If men fight, and hurt a woman with child, so that she gives birth prematurely, yet no lasting harm follows, he shall surely be punished accordingly as the woman's husband imposes on him; and he shall pay as the judges determine. But if any lasting harm follows, then you shall give life for life. (Ex. 21:22-23)

Abortion is not only a sin, but a crime, and, indeed, a capital crime.[5]

PERSONAL BENEFITS

1. God's Law outlines specific moral behavior, eliminating the guesswork from moral conduct. "Your word is a lamp to my feet and a light to my path" (Ps. 119:105). The Christian should not be one who gropes in darkness, but should be one who walks in the light (1 John 1:7).

2. It obligates us to treat with respect even our personal enemy. "If you meet your enemy's ox or his donkey going astray, you shall surely bring it back to him again. If you see the donkey of one who hates you lying under its burden, and you would refrain from helping it, you shall surely help him with it" (Ex. 23:4-5). Personal vengeance is reduced and stability enhanced when God's Law is held in high regard.

3. It obligates us to love our neighbor as ourselves. "You shall not take vengeance, nor bear any grudge against the children of your people, but you shall love

your neighbor as yourself: I am the LORD" (Lev. 19:18).

4. It obligates us to insure the safety of guests on our property. "When you build a new house, then you shall make a parapet for your roof, that you may not bring bloodguiltiness on your house if anyone falls from it" (Deut. 22:8; see also Ex. 21:33-34).

5. It obligates us to full financial remuneration to those whom we harm.

> If men contend with each other, and one strikes the other with a stone or with his fist, and he does not die but is confined to his bed, if he rises again and walks about outside with his staff, then he who struck him shall be acquitted. He shall only pay for the loss of his time, and shall provide for him to be thoroughly healed. (Ex. 21:18-19)

6. It forbids us to loan money at interest to a needy person.

> If you lend money to any of My people who are poor among you, you shall not be like a moneylender to him; you shall not charge him interest. If you ever take your neighbor's garment as a pledge, you shall return it to him before the sun goes down. For that is his only covering, it is his garment for his skin. What will he sleep in? And it will be that when he cries to Me, I will hear, for I am gracious. (Ex. 22:25-27)

NOTES

1. See also Ps. 119:44, 137, 142, 144.
2. See also Prov. 11:1; Isa. 1:22.

3. This indentured servitude would force the thief literally to pay for his crime.
4. See also vv. 7-9.
5. Kenneth L. Gentry, Jr., *The Christian Case Against Abortion*, 2d ed. (Memphis, Tenn.: Footstool, 1989), pp. 62-68.

CHAPTER EIGHT

CONCLUSION

Despite much confusion from detractors of theonomic ethics, the theonomic approach to moral conduct is not an attempt to offer a plan for works justification. Theonomy simply teaches that the Word of God is the supreme standard by which people will be judged. Having a revealed and objective standard takes the guesswork out of righteous living.

Neither does theonomy involve an attempt to force Christianity on a nation by raw political, judicial, or military power. Though God's Law sets the pattern for all of life (not just the inner personal sphere of human existence), the long-range implementation of God's Law must follow, not precede, massive Christian revival. Then a nation of judicially righteous people will seek a judicially righteous government according to the standard of God's righteousness, not fallen and sinful man's.

The Christian should understand that the only alternative to God's Law is man's law. There is no neutrality. Jesus said, "He who is not with Me is against Me" (Luke 11:23a), and "No servant can serve two masters; for either he will hate the one and love the other, or else he will be loyal to the one and despise the other" (Luke 16:13a). The Bible nowhere disestablishes God's Law, but everywhere affirms it. We should expect that God's Law continues into the New Testament era, unless there is a word from God in Scripture that disannuls it, either in precept or in practice. Whether God's Law is congenial to our personal feelings or our contemporary environment is not the issue for the Christian. That it is the binding and obligatory standard of God's justice is the sole issue.

Christianity has given birth to the greatest prosperity, stability, and liberty known in history. To the extent that the Christian view is also the biblical view (contrary to liberalism, which attempts to separate the two[1]), we may expect God's objective blessings upon that people whose God is the Lord, as evidenced in their law code.

The Christianity of the Bible provides a life-encompassing world view. True Christianity has an authoritative word from God for all of life.

> Therefore be careful to observe them; for this is your wisdom and your understanding in the sight of the peoples who will hear all these statutes, and say, "Surely this great nation is a wise and understanding people." For what great nation is there that has God so near to it, as the LORD our God is to us, for whatever reason we may call upon Him? And what great nation is there that

has such statutes and righteous judgments as are in all this law which I set before you this day? (Deut. 4:6-8)

Therefore the law is holy, and the commandment holy and just and good. (Rom. 7:12)

We know that the law is good if one uses it lawfully, knowing this: that the law is not made for a righteous person, but for the lawless and insubordinate, for the ungodly and for sinners, for the unholy and profane, for murderers of fathers and murderers of mothers, for manslayers, for fornicators, for sodomites, for kidnappers, for liars, for perjurers, and if there is any other thing that is contrary to sound doctrine, according to the glorious gospel of the blessed God which was committed to my trust. (1 Tim. 1:8-11)

NOTES

1. In his defense of the PCUSA special report on human sexuality in 1991, John Carey, chairman of the committee that wrote the report, commented, "Biblical ethics and Christian ethics for the church today are not the same thing" (Randy Frame, "Sexuality Report Draws Fire," *Christianity Today*, April 29, 1991, p. 37).

INDEX
OF
SCRIPTURE

8:66ff.—20
9:22—31
9:22–26—31

James
1:25—16
2:9—18, 38
2:10—18
2:10–12—38
3:6—20

1 Peter
1:19—47

2 Peter
2:9—54

1 John
1:7—64
2:3–4—38
2:4–6—30
3:4—17, 30
5:3—38

Revelation
15:4—16
20:12—38